D1366556

MORAY EELS

by Don P. Rothaus

The Child's World

Content Adviser:
Kristi Schultz, Instructor,
The Florida Aquarium

Published in the United States of America by The Child's World®
PO Box 326 • Chanhassen, MN 55317-0326
800-599-READ • www.childsworld.com

PHOTO CREDITS

© Brandon D. Cole: cover, 1, 6, 25
© Jeff Rotman/jeffrotman.com: 8, 18, 28
© Lawson Wood/Corbis: 10–11
© Louise Murray/Getty Images: 23
© Michael Patrick O'Neill/Photo Researchers, Inc.: 26
© Robert E. Barber/Alamy: 16–17
© Sinclair Stammers/Photo Researchers, Inc.: 21
© Stephen Frink/Corbis: 5, 12, 13, 15
© Wolfgang Pölzer/Alamy: 19

ACKNOWLEDGMENTS

The Child's World®: Mary Berendes, Publishing Director;
Katherine Stevenson, Editor

The Design Lab: Kathleen Petelinsek, Design and Page Production

LIBRARY OF CONGRESS CATALOGING-IN-PUBLICATION DATA

Rothaus, Don P.
  Moray eels / by Don P. Rothaus.
      p. cm. — (New naturebooks)
  Includes bibliographical references and index.
  ISBN 1-59296-644-6 (library bound : alk. paper)
  1. Morays—Juvenile literature. I. Title. II. Series.
  QL638.M875R68 2006
  597'.43—dc22   2006001372

Table of Contents

On the cover: This white-mouthed moray eel is peeking out of its coral home near Hawai'i's Kona Coast.

Meet the Moray Eel!

Moray eels have been around for about two million years.

As the divers swim toward the coral reef, they enter a world of color and beauty. Fish of all different shapes, sizes, and colors dart in and around the reef. The divers begin a careful search, shining their lights underneath ledges and into the reef's cracks and small caves.

The lights reveal all kinds of fish and shrimp that use these hiding places during the day. Finally, the divers find the object of their search. Their lights shine off the teeth of a large creature hidden within the reef, its head swaying in the lazy ocean **current**. What is this creature? It's a moray eel!

Green morays like this one grow to be about 10 feet (3 m) long. They are common in the warm waters off the coasts of North, Central, and South America.

What Are Moray Eels?

Moray eels swim by moving their bodies from side to side in an S pattern.

Morays are one of the few fish that can swim backward. That comes in handy for backing into holes in rocks or coral reefs.

Morays are eel-shaped fishes found mostly in the warmer waters of the world's oceans. They aren't true eels, because true eels have fins on their sides, and morays don't. Morays live around coral reefs and in rocky areas at depths of 5 to 150 feet (1.5 to 46 m). There are more than a hundred different kinds, or **species**, of morays. Green morays are the largest species, growing up to 10 feet (3 m) long. Pygmy morays are the smallest, growing to only about 8 inches (20 cm) long. Most moray species are about 5 feet (1.5 m) long and weigh about 40 pounds (18 kg).

Here you can see a spotted moray as it watches the photographer. Spotted morays live in the Atlantic Ocean, from North Carolina all the way to Brazil. Unlike most morays, spotted morays are active during the daytime rather than at night.

What Do Morays Look Like?

Green morays are actually dark blue. Their slimy mucus is yellow—which makes their blue color look green.

Morays have long, ribbon-shaped bodies. A **dorsal fin** runs the entire length of their back. Most fish have scales, but morays don't. Instead, they have thick, leathery skin covered with a slimy, protective coating called **mucus**. The mucus helps morays slip in and out of the rocky places where they live and hide. Without it, they would get lots of cuts and scrapes.

Other fish have dorsal and side fins that help them stay upright. Morays, however, have low dorsal fins and no side fins at all, so they tip over a lot. In fact, it's not uncommon to see morays drifting along on their sides—or even upside down!

This green moray is hunting at night in the Caribbean Sea. You can see its long, thin dorsal fin. What do you think this moray's skin would feel like if you touched it?

How can you tell different species of moray eels apart? By their sizes, the colors and patterns on their skin, and the areas of the world in which they live. Besides the green moray, some of the more common morays found near North America are the spotted moray, the California moray, the chain moray, and the goldentail moray.

A moray's coloring helps it blend in with its surroundings. This coloring, called **camouflage**, helps the moray hide from the animals it hunts.

Moray eels are sometimes called "painted eels" because some of them are so brightly colored. Many have stripes, speckles, or other bold patterns.

Because morays keep their mouths open, even the insides of their mouths have camouflage.

Geometric morays like this one get their name from the geometric pattern of dots on their heads. These morays live only in shallow areas of the western Indian Ocean.

11

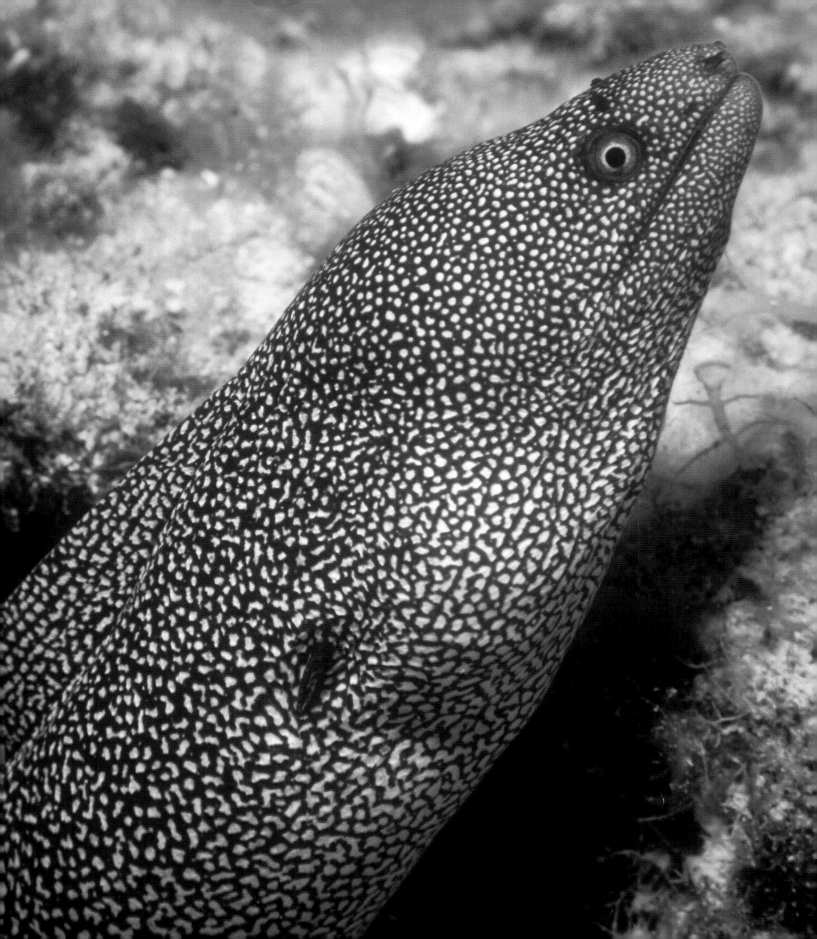

This panomic green moray isn't angry— it's simply opening its mouth to breathe.

Many people think moray eels are scary and dangerous. Perhaps that's because of how the morays look—and how they breathe. Like fish, morays breathe with **gills**. But morays' gill openings aren't like the skinny gill slits of fish. Instead, their gill openings are round. To breathe, the morays gulp water constantly. Their mouths slowly open and close—and never stop!

Many morays have sharp, thin, fanglike teeth. As the morays open and close their mouths, people might think the animals look angry or are getting ready to attack. The truth is, they're just breathing. Actually, morays are fairly shy animals.

Many moray eels have teeth not only in their upper and lower jaws, but also in the roofs of their mouths, to keep food from escaping.

Here you can see a goldentail moray as it peers out of its hiding place in the Caribbean Sea. You can see the round gill opening on its side.

13

What Do Moray Eels Eat?

Moray eels have an excellent sense of smell. Some morays even have four nostrils—two for long-range smelling and two for close-up!

Most moray species are **nocturnal**, which means they are active at night. During the daytime, a moray stays in its hiding place, or **lair**, remaining fairly still. When night falls, the moray leaves its lair in search of food. Morays are **predators**, which means they hunt and eat other animals. Many of the animals they eat, called their **prey**, are active during the day. The morays hunt them at night, when the animals are resting.

This green moray is hunting near a shipwreck off the coast of Bonaire Island, in the Caribbean Sea. You can see how it moves its body in an S shape as it swims along.

A moray finds its food by following smells. The tube-shaped nostrils on the front of its snout help it track down its prey. Fish are morays' favorite food, but some moray species also like octopus, mussels, clams, lobsters, and shrimp. Morays prefer live food, but if they are very hungry, they sometimes eat dead animals.

A moray's mouth can open both sideways and up and down, allowing the moray to eat larger foods.

This spotted moray eel is hunting off the coast of the Galápagos Islands. The moray is easy to see in this picture, but once the photographer turned off his light, the animal blended right in with the nearby rocks.

17

How Do Moray Eels Eat?

Morays can tie their bodies in knots to give themselves extra strength for tearing their food.

Morays use their fanglike teeth to catch and hold their prey. The teeth angle back toward the moray's throat, making it difficult for the captured animal to wiggle free. When a moray catches a fish, it often moves the fish around in its mouth so that it can swallow it headfirst. This keeps the sharp spines of the fish's dorsal fin from sticking into the moray's throat.

Morays' sharp fangs won't break through hard shells, though. So how do some moray species eat animals that have shells? These morays have pebblelike crushing teeth, called *pharyngeal* (fair-en-JEE-el) *teeth*, in their throats.

18

On this page you can see how sharp a giant moray's teeth are. On the facing page you can see a giant moray attacking a fish on the ocean floor near Indonesia.

What Are Baby Moray Eels Like?

Moray eggs are tiny—only about the size of a BB!

Moray eels like to live alone. But when the time comes to mate, morays leave their lairs to search for a partner. Morays mate far out in the ocean, where the female releases millions of eggs.

The eggs drift along on the ocean currents. About 10 weeks later, the eggs hatch, producing long, clear, ribbonlike **larvae**. The larvae float on the ocean currents and feed on tiny animals and plants known as **plankton**. As the tiny morays grow, they slowly begin to look more like adults. After about eight months, the young morays settle near coral reefs or rocky areas and make their first lairs.

This close-up photo shows baby eels starting to grow inside their eggs. You can clearly see their eyes and tails.

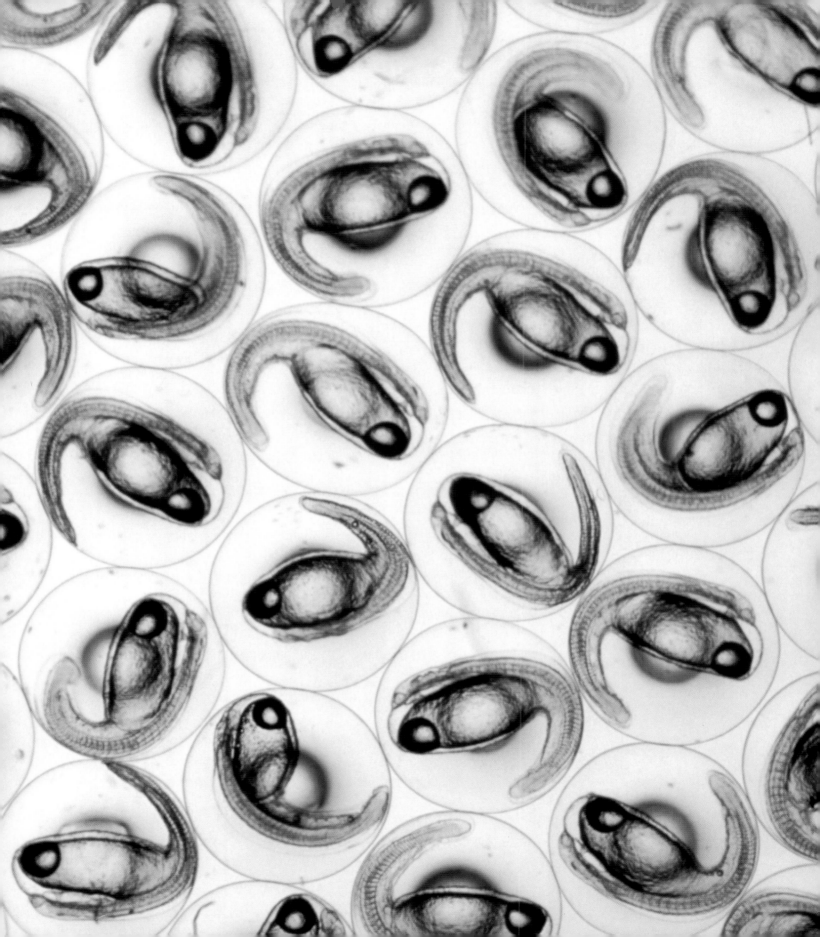

Are All Fish Afraid of Morays?

Cleaner wrasses are only about 4 inches (10 cm) long. These little helpers are important to almost every type of fish. Even sharks don't mind them!

Cleaner shrimp are only about 2 inches (5 cm) long. They stand in the open and dance to attract fish. Fish that need cleaning recognize the shrimp's "cleaning dance" and stop by.

To many other ocean creatures, moray eels are dangerous predators. But there are two animals that have no fear of morays. A tiny fish known as the *cleaner wrasse* (RASS) swims around the moray's face and body, feeding on **parasites**. The cleaner shrimp removes parasites, too, as it wanders along the edge of the moray's mouth and teeth.

This arrangement works well for everybody. The moray gets rid of annoying parasites. The cleaner wrasse and the cleaner shrimp get an easy meal.

This giant moray is being visited by both a cleaner wrasse and a cleaner shrimp. The cleaner wrasse is near the moray's eye and mouth. The cleaner shrimp is moving down from the top of the moray's head.

Are Moray Eels Dangerous?

Moray bites aren't common, but they can be severe. The moray's teeth cause ragged wounds that can become infected from the saliva in the eel's mouth.

For the most part, morays aren't dangerous to people. There are a few situations, however, in which they might bite. If somebody diving or fishing hurts or threatens a moray, the moray might bite to defend itself. A moray also might bite if a diver accidentally reaches into the moray's lair.

Dragon morays like this one are shy, but they can get nasty if they feel threatened. They get their name from the "horns" on their head, which remind many people of a dragon. They are common in ocean waters from Japan to Hawai'i.

Sometimes divers think its fun to feed morays by hand, but that can be risky! Morays have very bad eyesight, and they sometimes bite the diver by mistake. In fact, a human hand reaching into a moray's dark hiding place might look like a small octopus—one of the moray's favorite foods!

Moray eels sometimes make their lairs in objects made by people, such as pipes.

This yellow moray didn't like how close the photographer came to its lair!

Scuba divers around the world enjoy watching moray eels. In some areas, morays have become used to divers and will come out of their lairs to greet them. Like our own pets, some of these morays have even been given names! It's important to realize, however, that these graceful animals are not pets. They're wild animals that sometimes do things we don't expect. As long as divers approach morays with respect, move slowly, and act gently, morays and divers will continue to get along.

People don't usually eat moray eels, since their meat can be poisonous to humans.

Wild morays can live to be 30 years old.

These divers are getting a close-up view of a green moray that lives in a shipwreck. The curious moray came out to investigate, and the divers stayed still until it went back inside the ship.

Glossary

camouflage (KAM-oo-flazh) Camouflage is coloring or markings that help an animal blend in with their surroundings. Moray eels have camouflage—even in their mouths.

current (KUR-rent) An ocean current is a stream of water flowing in one direction. Moray eggs drift with the currents.

dorsal fin (DOR-sull FIN) A dorsal fin is located on a fish's back. Moray eels have a long, low dorsal fin.

gills (GILZ) Gills are organs that many underwater animals use to breathe. Moray eels breathe through gills.

lair (LAYR) A moray eel's lair is its home or hiding place. Morays make their lairs in coral reefs or rocky areas with deep holes or cracks.

larvae (LAR-vee) In some animals, larvae are the young, very different forms of the animals when they first hatch or are born. Moray eel larvae are long and clear.

mucus (MYOO-kuss) Mucus is a slimy coating that some animals make from their bodies. Moray eels are covered with mucus.

nocturnal (nok-TURN-ull) When an animal is nocturnal, it rests during the day and is active at night. Most moray eels are nocturnal.

parasites (PAYR-uh-sites) Parasites are animals that live on or inside other animals. Like most animals, moray eels have parasites.

plankton (PLANK-tun) Plankton are plants and animals that drift in the ocean. Most plankton are very tiny. Moray eel larvae eat plankton.

predators (PRED-uh-terz) Predators are animals that hunt and eat other animals. Morays are predators.

prey (PRAY) Prey are animals that eaten as food. Many types of fish are prey for moray eels.

species (SPEE-sheez) A species is a different kind of a certain animal. There are almost a hundred different species of moray eels.

To Find Out More

Read It!

Gross, Miriam J. *The Moray Eel.* New York: PowerKids Press, 2005.

Hirschmann, Kris. *Moray Eels.* San Diego, CA: KidHaven Press, 2003.

Stone, Lynn M. *Eels.* Vero Beach, FL: Rourke, 2005.

Wallace, Karen, and Mike Bostock (illustrator). *Think of an Eel.* Cambridge, MA: Candlewick Press, 2004.

On the Web

Visit our home page for lots of links about moray eels: *http://www.childsworld.com/links*

Note to Parents, Teachers, and Librarians: We routinely check our Web links to make sure they're safe, active sites—so encourage your readers to check them out!

31

Index

About the Author

Don Rothaus has a degree in zoology from the University of Washington. For the past 17 years he has been a biologist for the State of Washington, Department of Fish and Wildlife. His research centers on marine invertebrates, including sea urchins, sea cucumbers, geoduck clams, and abalone. He also enjoys participating in seasonal environmental education and outreach programs for elementary school classrooms in the greater Seattle area. Don is an avid diver and underwater photographer.